THE VOYAGE OF
THE BEAGLE

Kate Hyndley

Illustrated by Peter Bull

The Bookwright Press
New York · 1989

Great Journeys

The First Men on the Moon
The Race to the South Pole
The Travels of Marco Polo
The Voyage of the Beagle

Cover Charles Darwin's research during the expedition of the Beagle was to change the way scientists thought. This picture shows Darwin studying iguanas in their natural habitat on the Galápagos Islands.

Frontispiece Charles Darwin as a young man.

First published in the
United States in 1989 by
The Bookwright Press
387 Park Avenue South
New York, NY 10016

First published in 1989 by
Wayland (Publishers) Limited
61 Western Road, Hove
East Sussex BN3 1JD, England

© Copyright 1989 Wayland (Publishers) Limited

Typeset by DP Press Ltd, Sevenoaks, Kent
Printed in Italy by G. Canale & C.S.p.A., Turin

Library of Congress-in-Publication Data
Hyndley, Kate
    The Voyage of the Beagle /by Kate
Hyndley.
        p.   cm.—(Great journeys)
    Bibliography: p.
    Includes index.
    Summary: An account of the five
years that English naturalist Charles
Darwin spent traveling around the
world on the HMS Beagle, a voyage
that led him to develop his theory of the
evolution of the species.
    ISBN 0–531–18272–X
    1. Darwin, Charles, 1809–1882—
Juvenile literature. 2. Beagle
Expedition (1831–1836)—Juvenile
literature. 3. Naturalists–England—
Biography—Juvenile literature. [1.
Darwin, Charles, 1809–1882. 2. Beagle
Expedition (1831–1836). 3.
Naturalists.]
I. Title.   II. Series.
QH31.D2H96 1989
508'.092'4—dc19
[B]
[92]   88–28695
                                 CIP
                                 AC

Contents

A Great Adventure

In 1831 an invitation was sent to Charles Darwin. He was a young student at Cambridge at the time, twenty-two years old and rather bored with his life so far. He was invited to join HMS *Beagle* on a surveying trip around the world as the ship's naturalist.

The voyage of the *Beagle* was to change his life forever. In the five years that Darwin spent traveling around the world, he discovered many strange and wonderful animals: an inflatable fish, giant tortoises, singing frogs and many other amazing creatures. Twenty years after his return, Darwin published a book called *On the Origin of Species*. It contained a new idea about how the natural world worked: how different types of animals and plants had come to exist and how they had changed over hundreds and thousands of years. This book was to change forever our understanding of nature, and as a result of its publication Charles Darwin became a world-famous scientist.

The first twenty-one years of Darwin's life were quite uneventful. He was the son of a wealthy doctor and was brought up as a young gentleman. After attending boarding school,

Above *Charles's father, Dr. Robert Darwin.*

Below *While a student at Cambridge, Darwin began to collect and study specimens.*

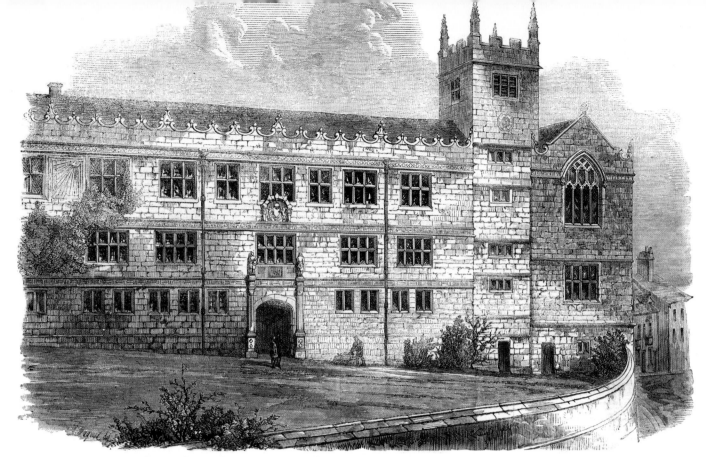

where he was not thought to be particularly smart, he went to Edinburgh to study medicine like his father had done earlier. This was not a success. He could not stand the sight of blood and suffering (operations were carried out without anesthetics in those days), and soon he left for Cambridge to study to become a clergyman. At Cambridge, Darwin was known as a friendly and popular young man who liked hunting, shooting and parties. He had just managed to pass his exams when he was offered the chance to join the *Beagle*.

Although Darwin did not seem particularly smart at school or at the university, he had always been interested in nature. From an early age he had been fascinated by the flowers, birds, insects and other animals he saw around him. He knew the names of many animals by the time he was eight years old and, as he grew older, he began to collect specimens of different insects as a hobby. At Cambridge he had a large collection of beetles, which he kept in his room. However, he had never intended to make a career of studying nature, so he was surprised and very excited when he was offered the post of ship's naturalist on the *Beagle*.

The offer came from Captain Robert Fitzroy who was to lead the expedition. It was important that Fitzroy and Darwin should like each other as they would have to share a cabin for the next five years. On September 5, 1831 Darwin traveled to London to meet Captain Fitzroy for the first time.

Above left *A contemporary engraving of Shrewsbury Grammar School, which Charles Darwin attended as a boy.*

Fitzroy and the *Beagle*

When Captain Fitzroy first met Charles Darwin in his London club, he liked him immediately. Darwin was an enthusiastic and cheerful young man and was easy to get along with. Fitzroy's only worry was that Darwin might not be strong enough for the long voyage.

Fitzroy came from an aristocratic family and was very proud and strict. He was only twenty-six, but this was to be his second voyage as commander of the *Beagle*. Although he was

Below *The* Beagle *was a small ship, but it was very adaptable.*

brave and generous he also had a terrible temper, and his crew was careful not to upset him. Captain Fitzroy had very strong ideas about right and wrong. He was a very religious man and believed every word that was written in the Bible. He hoped that, on their journey, Darwin would be able to find some proof in nature that what was written in the Bible about the beginning of the world was true.

Captain Fitzroy explained the purpose of their voyage to Darwin. They were to make detailed maps of the coast of South America and to take scientific measurements around

Above
Captain Robert Fitzroy.

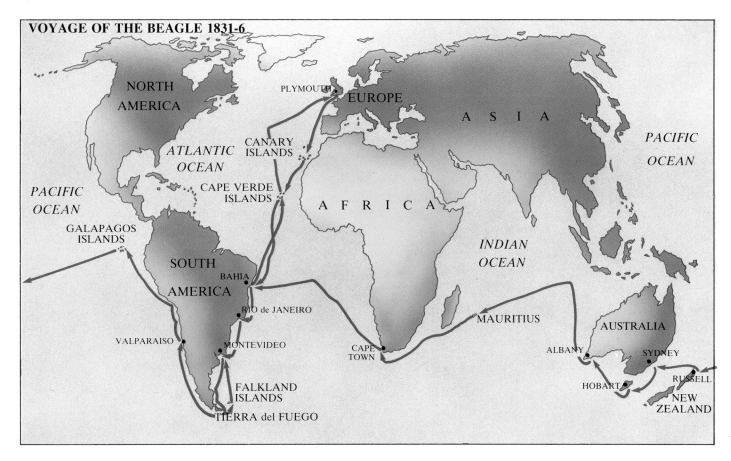

VOYAGE OF THE BEAGLE 1831-6

NORTH AMERICA

PLYMOUTH

EUROPE

ASIA

PACIFIC OCEAN

ATLANTIC OCEAN

CANARY ISLANDS

PACIFIC OCEAN

CAPE VERDE ISLANDS

AFRICA

GALAPAGOS ISLANDS

INDIAN OCEAN

SOUTH AMERICA

BAHIA

RIO de JANEIRO

MAURITIUS

AUSTRALIA

VALPARAISO

MONTEVIDEO

CAPE TOWN

ALBANY

SYDNEY

FALKLAND ISLANDS

RUSSELL

HOBART

TIERRA del FUEGO

NEW ZEALAND

the world, which would make maps more accurate. Fitzroy invited Darwin to go with him to see the *Beagle* at Plymouth where she was being refitted. She was a small ship, only 90 ft (27 m) long and weighing 242 tons. Darwin thought she was very well fitted out; everything was made of mahogany. There would not be much space, however, as there would be 74 people on board. Besides Fitzroy and Darwin there were six other officers, a doctor, his assistant and an artist.

Now that he had seen the ship, Darwin was very excited about the voyage. He set off immediately to say goodbye to his family and to pack his clothes and equipment. He took with him a microscope,

a compass, a book on taxidermy, binoculars, a magnifying glass and jars of spirits for preserving specimens. Fitzroy took Darwin to buy guns as it would not be safe to go ashore without them in many of the places the ship would be visiting. He bought a case of pistols and a rifle.

At last, on December 27, 1831, the *Beagle* set sail from Plymouth. Darwin liked life on board ship but was very seasick. He suffered from this illness throughout the whole trip and had to lie in his hammock eating only raisins when the weather was bad. As they sailed closer to the South American coast, the sea grew calmer and Darwin was able to go on deck and see the strange birds and sea creatures around the ship.

Above *This map shows the route taken by Captain Fitzroy and marks the main places that the* Beagle *visited.*

The Forests of Brazil

As soon as the *Beagle* arrived at Salvador in Brazil, Darwin went ashore to explore. He was amazed at the beauty of the tropical forests. The huge trees were covered with creepers and surrounded by thickly growing plants. The air was warm and steamy and there were brilliantly colored birds and flowers all around. Darwin thought the forests were like paradise.

Walking along the shore one day, Darwin discovered a very strange fish called a Diodon. When it was in danger it would fill itself up with water and air until it was round like a balloon. It could protect itself by biting, or by squirting water at its enemies. Several inflated fish had been found alive inside the stomach of a shark. Inflated fish had also been found to have

eaten their way out of a shark and killed it. Darwin wrote in his diary, "Who would ever have imagined that a soft little fish could have destroyed the great and savage shark?"

Soon after this discovery, the *Beagle* sailed south to Rio de Janeiro in Brazil. From here Darwin set off on an expedition inland to visit a coffee-growing estate. They rode for several days through forests and grasslands. On the way they

Below *Darwin explored dense forests in Brazil and saw many beautiful creatures, including brightly colored birds and bearded monkeys.*

passed some huge conical ants' nests that were nearly 12 feet (4 m) high. The creepers were so thick in some places that a man was sent ahead with a sword to cut a path through them.

The coffee estates were run by slave owners. Slavery was very common in South America at this time. Darwin hated the cruel way that the slaves were treated. When he finally left Brazil he wrote, "I thank God I shall never again visit a slave country . . . I have seen a little boy, six or seven years old, struck thrice with a horsewhip (before I could interfere) on his naked head, for having handed me a glass of water not quite clean."

When they returned to Rio de Janeiro, Darwin was invited to go hunting in the forest. The hunting party shot two large bearded monkeys. These animals have very strong tails that will support their whole weight. One of the monkeys was still holding on to a branch with its tail even after it had been killed. The hunters had to cut down the tree to get hold of it.

In the evenings Darwin liked to sit and listen to the sounds of the forest. There were some little frogs that seemed to sing different notes together so that it sounded like harmony. He also liked to watch the brightly colored fireflies shining in the dark. For several months Darwin was happy exploring the forests and observing and collecting all the new animals and plants he found there. In July the *Beagle* was ready to sail south again.

Living with the Gauchos

Leaving the harbor at Rio de Janeiro bound for Montevideo, the *Beagle* was surrounded by a huge school of porpoises playing in the water. One night the sailors saw many seals and penguins around the ship.

When he arrived at Montevideo, Darwin packed up some of the specimens he had collected to send back to England. The birds and other larger animals had been stuffed, while insects and other smaller animals had been preserved in spirits. Among his collection were eighty kinds of birds, nine types of snakes and many other types of reptiles.

For the next two years the *Beagle* traveled up and down the east coast of South America, surveying the coastline and making maps. Darwin spent some of the time on the ship but also went on many inland excursions. In September 1833 he traveled 400 miles (644 km) from Bahia Blanca to Buenos Aires on horseback with gauchos as his guides.

Gauchos were cowboys who lived and worked on the huge plains called the Pampas. Darwin was very impressed by the wild, elegant and very skillful gauchos. They were tall and handsome, with long black hair curling down their backs. They wore long white boots, wide trousers and scarlet sashes. In the evenings they drank and smoked cigars and,

although they were very polite, they always carried their daggers with them. Darwin wrote, "The gaucho, although he may be a cutthroat, is a gentleman."

The gauchos were cattlemen, and they used two main tools in their work: the lasso and the bolas. The lasso was a long thin rope made of braided leather with a loop at one end. The bolas (or balls) were two or three round rocks covered with leather joined together with a leather strap. When they were spun and thrown, an animals legs would be wound together.

One day Darwin was riding along spinning the bolas above his head when one of the balls became caught on a bush. As the other ball dropped to the ground it wound around one of the horse's hind legs and the animal was tied to the bush. Darwin

Above Darwin was excited to see schools of porpoises following the Beagle *as it left the harbor of Rio de Janeiro. Porpoises seemed to enjoy swimming in the wake of the ship and followed it for a long time, hoping to gather food from the waste thrown overboard.*

Opposite right The gauchos were very skilled horsemen. When they wanted to catch one of their cattle, they would use the bolas.

described how they laughed at him, "The gauchos roared with laughter; they cried out that they had seen every sort of animal caught, but had never before seen a man caught by himself."

On their trip across the Pampas, Darwin and the gauchos lived in the open, sometimes eating armadillos roasted in their shells on the fire. The gauchos once killed a puma to eat and found an ostrich nest containing 27 eggs inside its stomach. For several days at a time they ate only meat (which Darwin hated).

When they reached Buenos Aires, Darwin found that the crew of the *Beagle* had not yet finished its work.

Above *The gauchos often ate the meat of armadillos, which they roasted in their shells.*

Dinosaurs and Indians

Darwin made one of his most exciting discoveries at a place called Punta Alta. While digging in the gravel and shingle, the explorers began to uncover large fossilized bones. Not only did the bones belong to animals that had died out a long time ago but they were of an enormous size. Working with pickaxes, they managed to unearth the fossilized skeletons of nine huge land animals. As the fossils were all found on the beach within a space of 200 square yards, Darwin soon realized that at one time these animals must have existed in large numbers.

Among the fossils Darwin found there and in other areas were the skeletons of a megatherium, a huge sloth-like animal that fed on leaves, a mastodon, similar to an elephant, and a glyptodont, like a giant armadillo. When the soil had been scraped out of it, the fossilized shell of the glyptodont looked like a huge cauldron.

Darwin wondered how these animals had died out and he discussed this problem with Fitzroy. Fitzroy believed the explanation of the Creation that was written in the Bible. This was that God made the world and all the animals in it in six days. When humankind became evil, God sent a flood to destroy the world and saved only Noah and his Ark full of animals.

Below *Darwin unearthed the fossilized bones of prehistoric creatures on a beach near Montevideo. Among the remains he found were the bones of a mastodon and those of a glyptodont.*

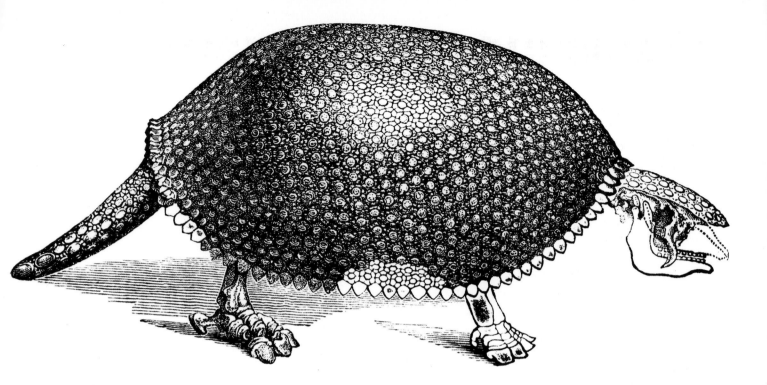

Fitzroy believed that the animals that had died out were those that had not been saved in the Ark by Noah.

Darwin doubted this theory, especially when he found more fossils at Santa Fe, 300 miles (483 km) from Buenos Aires. Among these remains was the fossilized tooth of a horse. Darwin was fascinated by this, because when the Spanish arrived in South America in 1535 there had been no horses. They had been introduced by the Spanish colonists, and this animal, which had died out millions of years earlier, began to live and breed in South America again.

When Darwin brought the huge fossilized bones on board the *Beagle* he was teased for making the decks untidy. The crew were amazed at the "rubbish" he brought on board.

On all his expeditions in this region Darwin had known of the danger of being attacked by South American Indians. The Spanish were at war with the Indians, whose civilization they were attempting to destroy. There was much cruelty on both sides, but Darwin sympathized with the Indians. He described how one Indian chief and his little son escaped from an attack by clinging to the side of a horse, with one arm around its neck and one leg lodged on its back, to avoid the soldiers' rifle shots.

Darwin did not think that the Indians had much future. "I think there will not, in another half century, be a wild Indian northward of the Rio Negro. The warfare is too bloody to last; the Christians killing every Indian, and the Indians doing the same by the Christians. It is melancholy to trace how the Indians have given way before the Spanish invaders."

Above *Darwin found the remains of a glyptodont. Its shell was strong and domed, like that of a giant tortoise.*

The Land of Fire

The *Beagle* now sailed south again to the tip of South America, which was known as Tierra del Fuego (the Land of Fire). Fitzroy and Darwin visited this place at the end of 1832 and again in May 1834. On their first visit they met a group of friendly native people. They wore no clothes and their faces were painted black and red with white circles around their eyes. They were delighted when the sailors danced a hornpipe for them. The landscape was impressive but not very welcoming with its huge mountains and deep, dark forests. The climate was very cold and wet.

Captain Fitzroy had wanted to sail around Cape Horn to the west coast of Tierra del Fuego because he had promised to take three passengers back to their own people who lived there. These passengers were from Tierra del Fuego and had been taken to England by Fitzroy on his first visit three years earlier. Their names were York Minster, Jemmy Button and Fuegia Basket. Fitzroy had taught them to speak English, instructed them in his religion, and they now behaved like Europeans. He had promised to take them back to their families where he hoped they would pass on what they had learned to their own people. However, although the *Beagle* spent

Below The Fuegians lived in huts made of branches and bark. They were very hardy and lived without much clothing in the cold and rain of Tierra del Fuego.

Above *Captain Fitzroy had taken three Fuegians to Britain with him on his first voyage. During this expedition, he took them back to their homeland in small boats that he sailed through the Beagle Channel.*

twenty-four days at sea off Cape Horn, the ship was unable to reach the west coast because of the continuous gales. The *Beagle* had to return to harbor and wait for better weather.

Here they saw more closely the lifestyle of the Fuegians. They lived in huts that did little to keep out the cold, and they often slept on the wet ground with nothing to cover them. Despite the extreme cold they wore no clothes. They ate shellfish, gulls' eggs and fish from the sea, but in the winter they often starved. In bad winters they would kill and eat the old women in their camps before they harmed their hunting dogs. Their lives were very cruel. Darwin called Tierra del Fuego an "inhospitable and miserable" land.

Fitzroy decided to take York Minster, Jemmy Button and Fuegia Basket back to their families in small boats. They sailed through the Beagle Channel, which Fitzroy had

discovered on his earlier trip. All along the narrow channel, fires were lit by the Fuegians to spread the news of the white men's approach. The party from the *Beagle* were met by large numbers of curious Fuegians who continually begged them for presents. Darwin found this very irritating.

At last they reached the place where they could settle Fitzroy's Fuegian passengers. The crew put up tents for them, dug vegetable gardens and hoped they would settle happily. Later, when Fitzroy and Darwin returned, they found that it had not been easy for the Fuegians to go back to their homeland. They were not accepted by their own people until they looked and behaved just as they had done before they left. Darwin felt Fitzroy's experiment had been a failure because it had made living in a simple way more difficult for them and they had not influenced the other Fuegians at all.

Earthquake at Concepcion

Darwin was pleased to leave Tierra del Fuego, and in July 1834 the *Beagle* sailed up the west coast of South America to Valparaíso, the main sea port of Chile. Here the climate felt very warm and dry after the rigors of Tierra del Fuego, and Darwin began to enjoy himself again. At Valparaíso he was able to stay with an old school friend, and he spent his time riding out into the surrounding countryside to explore. Valparaíso means "valley of paradise." It had many orchards and green valleys, and Darwin found it to be very beautiful.

In the mountains around Valparaíso there were many gold and copper mines. The mines were simple and used little machinery; in some, the water was removed by men who carried it up the shaft in leather bags. At one gold mine Darwin observed the hard lives of the miners who seemed very pale. The mine was 450 feet (137 m) deep, and each man had to carry a load of rock weighing 200 pounds (91 kg). They carried this load as they climbed up notches cut in tree trunks that had been placed across the mine shaft. Their diet was boiled

Below *Darwin and Captain Fitzroy witnessed the aftermath of a terrible earthquake when they arrived at Concepcion.*

beans and bread. Although working conditions were very bad in the mines, the miners accepted them because the life of farmworkers was far worse.

After four months in Valparaíso, the *Beagle* sailed south again. In February 1835 a huge earthquake struck. Darwin and Fitzroy were near the island of Chiloé and only felt a shaking of the ground, but when they arrived at a large city called Concepcion, south of Valparaíso, they found it in ruins. The harbor had been destroyed, and debris from the smashed ships lay all along the shore. In the town, no houses were left standing, and seventy villages nearby were also ruined. Darwin found enormous cracks in the ground a yard (1 m) wide. Fortunately, the earthquake happened in the morning and people were able to run out of their houses before they collapsed. For this reason, the earthquake killed only a hundred people out of several thousand inhabitants. The huge cathedral was completely devastated and only parts of its north wall were left standing.

Shortly after the first shock, the water in the bay drew back leaving large ships aground for several minutes. Out at sea a huge wave began to gather. When this wave struck the shore it caused even more damage and loss of life. Luckily, most people had managed to escape to nearby hills.

Darwin was very interested in the effect the earthquake had on the level of the land. "The most remarkable effect of this earthquake was the permanent elevation of the land . . . There can be no doubt that the land around the Bay of Concepcion was upraised two or three feet." Soon after this the *Beagle* returned to Valparaíso for another six months.

Across the Andes

In March 1835, Darwin set off from Valparaíso to travel across the vast Cordillera range of the Andes. These magnificent mountains, parallel to the west coast of South America, spread north to south like a backbone. For a long time Darwin had wanted to explore these mountains and this was his first opportunity. Unlike Fitzroy, who thought the Andes had been created by God and had remained unchanged since the beginning of time, Darwin was full of curiosity about how the range had come to be there.

Darwin traveled with a guide, ten mules and a madrina. The madrina (which means godmother) was a female mule who led the others; they would follow the sound of her bell anywhere. The party had to carry a lot of food because there was a danger of being snowed in at this time of year. As they climbed higher, plants became more scarce and there were hardly any animals. The rocks were veined with silver, copper and gold, and there were mines in very remote places.

At 13,000 feet (4,000 m) the thin air made breathing difficult. The men felt a tightness in their chests and across their foreheads and quickly became short of breath and exhausted. Some of the men

Below Darwin and his party traveled through the Cordillera range in the Andes. High up in the mountains, the air was thin, and breathing became difficult.

found this very uncomfortable, but Darwin's mind was completely taken up by a discovery of fossilized shells. A find of fossil shells so high up meant that at one time even these high mountains had been under the ocean. Darwin had read the British geologist Charles Lyell who held the (then) unusual opinion that over millions of years there had been many changes in the level of the earth. Now Darwin was convinced that Lyell was right.

One evening the explorers tried to cook potatoes for supper, but because of the low air pressure the water boiled at a temperature much lower than usual. Although the potatoes had been boiling on the fire for several hours, they remained as hard as ever. This was because the water was actually quite cool even though it appeared to be boiling.

Passing through a snow-covered valley high up in the mountains, they saw an amazing sight. On a column of ice they clearly saw a frozen horse with its hind legs straight up in the air. Darwin thought that it must have fallen head-first into a hole in deep snow and, after the surrounding snow thawed, the horse had been left encased in ice.

After the party reached Mendoza they returned to Valparaíso by a different route. It was on the way back that Darwin found a group of trees that had been turned to stone. They were fir trees that had once stood on the edge of the

Atlantic Ocean, now over 600 miles (1,000 km) away. The trees had later been submerged by the ocean as the land level dropped. Now they were part of a mountain range 7,000 feet (2,000 m) high and had been changed into stone. Darwin was very excited to find this proof for Lyell's theory that the level of the land changes over the centuries.

When he returned to Valparaíso, the *Beagle* was ready to sail to Lima in Peru.

Above *Darwin discovered the remains of trees that had turned to stone over the centuries. These provided evidence to support Lyell's theory concerning changing land levels.*

The Galápagos Islands

In September 1835 the *Beagle* left Lima to sail west across the Pacific Ocean. The party intended to return to England by sailing around the Cape of Good Hope at the southern tip of Africa. Their first port of call was a group of islands 600 miles (1,000 km) west of Peru called the Galápagos Islands.

At first sight, the islands were not very attractive – black volcanic rocks sticking up from the sea with only a few scorched bushes growing on them. Darwin soon realized that the islands had once been underwater volcanoes, which had now risen above sea level. He stepped onto the beach to explore and found that the black sand was so hot that it burned his feet even through thick boots. The seashore was littered with tortoise shells. These had been left by whalers, who killed large numbers of tortoises.

The islands were inhabited by strange and interesting creatures. The word *galápagos* means giant tortoise in Spanish, and these huge animals thrived on the islands. Some were so large that it took eight men to lift one of them. One tortoise could provide 200 pounds (91 kg) of meat. Darwin walked inland to a spring where he watched the tortoises drink greedily. Sometimes they would drink only once a month. He tried riding on their backs but found it difficult to keep his balance. The crew ate tortoise meat. "While staying in this upper region we lived entirely on tortoise meat: the breast plate roasted with the flesh on it is very good; and the young tortoises make excellent soup; but otherwise the meat to my taste is indifferent," Darwin

Left *The Galápagos Islands are formed from volcanic rock. The wildlife living on these islands is highly varied and exotic.*

Right Among the strange creatures observed by Darwin were marine iguanas. They basked on the volcanic rocks and ate seaweed.

Above Giant tortoises can weigh far more than a human. They provided the expedition with an unusual and abundant source of fresh meat.

wrote. He also observed that on each island the tortoises had different shell markings.

On the beaches lived black lizards that were about 3 feet (1 m) long. They could swim well but never stayed in the sea for long. These sea-living lizards ate seaweed. The land-living lizards were more brightly colored and fed on cactus. They were very gentle animals and did not attack or bite anything, even when provoked.

There were a great many birds on the islands. Darwin did not need to use his gun at all because they were so unafraid of humans. The existence of all these different animals had a special importance for Darwin. Most of the creatures he saw lived only in the Galápagos Islands. They had adapted to the specific conditions on each island, and this demonstrated to Darwin the way in which plants and animals gradually change all over the world.

The different kinds of finches that lived on the islands provided another example of adaptation and change. Although all these little birds looked similar, their beaks were a different shape on each island. The shape of the beak depended on the type of food available. On one island the finches had strong thick beaks for cracking nuts, but on other islands they needed beaks of a different shape to feed on fruit. Darwin was very excited by this discovery. He wrote in his journal, "Both in space and time, we seem to be brought somewhat nearer to that great fact – that mystery of mysteries – the first appearance of new beings on this earth."

Tahiti and New Zealand

As the *Beagle* sailed on toward the tropical island of Tahiti, the crew felt relaxed and happy. Their work was done and they were going home. The wind blew them swiftly onward and the weather was warm and pleasant. The *Beagle* entered the harbor of Tahiti and was greeted by a fleet of canoes filled with cheerful Tahitians.

Their welcome continued when the crew went ashore and the men were all very impressed by the happy, friendly people who lived on the island. Their bodies were covered with tattoos in intricate patterns. The designs they used had changed with each generation. The young men had lines like those on a palm leaf curling around their bodies, but the old men had many tiny figures tattooed on their feet so that they looked as if they were wearing socks.

Tahiti itself was a beautiful island. A coral reef surrounded it. This meant that the water close to the shore was calm and still, like a lake. Many palm trees grew near the coast, and banana, orange, coconut and breadfruit trees grew everywhere on the island. Inland, fields were planted with yams, sugarcane and pineapples. The Tahitians lived on these fruits, which were plentiful.

Below *The crew of the* Beagle *relaxed on the sandy beaches of Tahiti, while Darwin led an expedition into the mountains.*

Above *Darwin was fascinated to watch Tahitians diving for fish. The food was wrapped in banana leaves and cooked between hot stones to make a delicious meal.*

Darwin asked two Tahitians to accompany him as guides on a trip into the mountains at the center of the island. Although he told them to take food and clothing for the journey, the Tahitians insisted that it was unnecessary. There was plenty of food in the mountains and their skin was all the clothing they would need. When evening came, the guides made supper. First they caught fish from a pool by diving in and following the fish until they had trapped them in crevices. They made a fire by rubbing the end of one stick into a groove in another, and when the wood began to burn, they placed round stones in the fire. Then they put the food wrapped in banana leaves between two layers of stones and covered the fire with earth so no heat could escape. In fifteen minutes a meal of fish, banana and wild arum was ready.

One evening Captain Fitzroy invited Queen Pomarre of Tahiti to visit the ship. There was food, singing, dancing and a display of fireworks to entertain the guests. In the morning the *Beagle* set sail for New Zealand.

New Zealand was a disappointment after Tahiti. Darwin thought that the people who lived there were dirty, and cruel to their slaves, and he did not like the tattoos they wore on their faces. He liked one custom of theirs however – rubbing noses as a greeting instead of shaking hands.

The English settlers in New Zealand had planted gardens that looked like those of English country cottages, where they grew roses and honeysuckle. This made Darwin feel very homesick. They stayed in New Zealand for only nine days and most of the crew felt this was quite long enough.

Australia

Australia was the next stop for the *Beagle*. In January 1836 they sailed into the harbor at Sydney. Darwin thought Sydney was a fine town with its many elegant houses, a good selection of shops and wide, clean streets. Many settlers who had come to Australia were becoming wealthy and building large new houses.

The countryside around Sydney was disappointing for Darwin. Eucalyptus trees were the only things that grew there, and they were pale and uninteresting and provided very little shade from the burning sun. The animals he had hoped to see were few in number, for they had been driven into more remote parts of the bush. One day they hunted for kangaroos and they did not see a single animal although they rode all day. Traveling through the country was easy (apart from the heat), since excellent roads had been built by the chain gangs. Australia was a penal colony, and chain gangs were groups of convicts who were forced to work, chained together and guarded by an overseer with a gun. Darwin also saw farms run by convicts. He disapproved of this as it seemed to him to be little different from slavery.

He enjoyed meeting a group of Aborigines who showed him their skills in spear throwing and animal tracking. Darwin found it surprising that they led a wandering life, and he could not understand why they did not settle and grow food. The Aborigines were becoming fewer and fewer. Many died from diseases brought to the continent by Europeans, and many suffered as the wild

Above A nineteenth-century illustration of Sydney Harbor.

Below Eucalyptus trees seemed to grow everywhere in Australia.

animals they hunted were driven away by the settlers. Darwin felt that the Aborigines would not have much future in Australia. He wrote, "Wherever the European has trod, death seems to pursue the Aboriginal."

The *Beagle* then left Australia bound for Keeling Island. This consists of a group of lagoon islands surrounded by coral reefs. There were coconut trees everywhere, and many animals, even the pigs, ate coconuts. Darwin was surprised to discover a coconut-eating crab whose claws could cut open the hard shell to reach the food inside. To show how strong the crab's claws were, one was shut in a cookie tin with the lid held on with wire. The crab managed to escape quite easily.

The existence of coral reefs in the middle of the ocean fascinated Darwin. Although the reef stood only a few feet above the water level and was constantly battered by the waves, it remained undamaged. He knew that the coral was made by millions of tiny sea animals called polyps and that it was constantly being replaced as the sea wore it away. But he also knew that the polyps could not live more than 120 feet (37 m) below the sea, so he decided that the reefs must be based on rocks. Darwin wrote many scientific papers about the coral reefs when he returned to England.

Below Darwin studied coral reefs during the expedition. He published the findings of his research on his return to Britain. This is the Great Barrier Reef in Australia.

The Journey Home

The crew of the *Beagle* was now suffering badly from home-sickness, and Darwin was one of the worst of the sufferers. They traveled back via Mauritius and Ascension Island, both of which were beautiful but of little interest except as stopping places bringing them closer to home. At last on October 2, 1836 the *Beagle* sailed into Falmouth. They had been away for nearly five years.

Darwin was so anxious to see his family again that he immediately boarded a coach for Shrewsbury. Travel was slow in those days, and, despite his eagerness, he did not arrive at his father's house until two days later. His father and sisters were very pleased to see him. They thought he was quite different in appearance. Darwin was very happy that his dog remembered him, and they set off on their usual walk as if he had never been away. Although Darwin lived until he was 73 years old, he never left England again. This was partly because for the rest of his life his health was never good. He was not strong enough to walk far or to work for more than a few hours a day on his scientific papers. The cause of his illness was unknown, but it was suspected that he might have caught a disease from an insect bite while on his travels.

For three years after his return Darwin lived in

Above *Emma Darwin.*

Left *Charles Darwin.*

Above Darwin's study in Down House, Kent.

Below On arrival at Falmouth, Darwin caught a stage coach to his home in Shrewsbury.

Cambridge and London, studying all the samples he had sent back to England and writing an account of his travels. His book, *Journal of the Voyage of the Beagle*, was published in 1839.

At the beginning of 1839 Darwin married his cousin Emma, whom he had known since childhood. They were very happy together and had ten children. Darwin was a very affectionate father. If one of his children became ill, he would wrap the child in a blanket on a sofa in his study so that he could talk to the child while he worked. Toward the end of his life Darwin wrote a book about his life for his family to read. About his children he says, "I have indeed been most happy in my family, and I must say to you my children that not one of you has ever given me one minute's anxiety, except on the score of health . . . When you were very young it was my delight to play with you all, and I think with a sigh that such days can never return."

In 1842 the Darwins moved away from London to a large house in Kent called Down House. In this peaceful place Darwin worked on his papers and books for the rest of his life. His main work, *On the Origin of Species*, was not published until 1859, more than twenty years after his return from the voyage of the *Beagle*. It sold out on the first day of publication and caused a great deal of argument because the ideas it contained were so revolutionary.

The Legacy of Darwin

Why did Darwin's work make people so angry? It was mainly a question of religion. Most people in Victorian England believed that God had created the world in six days. As God's world was created perfect, there had been no need for any change. Darwin argued that this was not true and that the natural world was changing all the time. Each type of plant or animal was slowly adapting – in a process known as "evolution."

Darwin noticed that animals produced more offspring than could possibly survive. This observation led him to the theory of "natural selection," which held that only the fittest creatures lived to reproduce their own kind. The fittest animals were not necessarily stronger or fiercer than the others. They were the ones that were best suited to their environment. In the same way as animal breeders can alter the characteristics of the creatures they breed, so nature has a way of adapting animals to their particular environment. Those that do not adapt simply die out.

The finches that Darwin saw on the Galápagos Islands illustrate adaptation. The birds had all started from a common ancestor. Those that had survived on each individual island were the ones that happened to have beaks shaped to eat the food available there. The finches whose beaks had the wrong shape for the food on that particular island had starved, while the birds that had adapted to suit the conditions there, thrived and reproduced.

Below *Diagram of Darwin's theory that humans and apes evolved from a common ancestor. Scientific thought today closely follows his theory.*

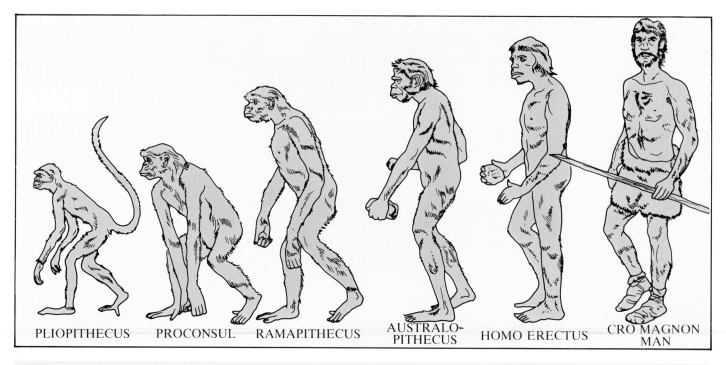

PLIOPITHECUS   PROCONSUL   RAMAPITHECUS   AUSTRALO-PITHECUS   HOMO ERECTUS   CRO MAGNON MAN

1 *2*

3 *4*

Above *This contemporary illustration shows the differently shaped beaks of various types of Galápagos finches. These birds provide a good example of natural adaptation. They have evolved beaks that are shaped to suit the particular type of food available in their habitats.*

Their offspring inherited beaks shaped like those of their parents, and in this way, a new type of bird gradually evolved.

The real problems began when people realized that Darwin's theory could mean that humans had also changed. He had not mentioned this idea in *On the Origin of Species* and Darwin did not write about human evolution until 1871, when *The Descent of Man* was published. It then became clear that he thought that humans and apes were descended from a common ancestor. This is an idea that we now accept quite readily, but in those days people were very insulted by the suggestion.

Gradually, Darwin's ideas were accepted and he became widely respected. When he died in 1882, he was buried in Westminster Abbey in London. His voyage on the *Beagle* had given him the opportunity to observe a huge variety of living things in their natural environment, and from this he developed a theory that changed our understanding of natural history forever.

Glossary

Aborigine One of the original inhabitants of Australia. The aborigines are the first people known to have lived in a particular place.

Adapted Changed so as to become better suited to a particular environment or way of life.

Anesthetic A drug or gas that is used to block the sensation of pain during surgery.

Ark The boat described in the Bible, in which Noah and his family and two of every kind of animal were saved from the flood.

Armadillo A burrowing animal with an armor of bony plates that covers its body.

Clergyman A minister, priest, rabbi, etc.

Conical Formed in the shape of a cone.

Coral reef A ridge just about even with the surface of the water, made of the skeletons of tiny marine animals called polyps.

Evolution The changes in the world of nature that occur in gradual stages.

Fossil The remains of a plant or an animal that have been preserved in rocks or bogs since prehistoric times.

Hammock A hanging bed made of rope and canvas that was used on board ships.

Harmony Two or more musical notes that make a pleasant sound when they are heard in combination.

Hornpipe A lively dance played and performed by sailors.

Lagoon A shallow lake that is often situated on the seashore and is separated from the sea itself by sand banks.

Mahogany A hard reddish-brown wood that is often used in expensive furniture. The wood comes from a tropical American tree.

Natural history The study of animals and plants.

Naturalist Someone who studies the world of nature, especially in their natural environment.

Natural selection The way in which certain types of plants or animals survive while others die out.

Polyps Very small and simple water animals. Corals are polyps that live in large groups.

Puma A cougar, a large animal of the cat family..

Reptile An animal with cold blood that has a backbone and crawls on its belly or creeps along the ground on short legs.

Sash A band of material that is worn over the shoulder or around the waist.

Slave Someone who is owned by another person. A slave works without being paid and is kept as a prisoner. Slaves were often bought by rich men to do particularly hard physical tasks or to work as unpaid servants.

Specimens Preserved examples of a particular kind of animal or plant.

Surveying The process of inspecting and reporting on the shape and size of a certain area, such as a particular coastline.

Survival of the fittest Theory that those animals best adapted to their particular environment will be the most likely to survive and reproduce.

Tattoo A picture in ink that is permanently picked into someone's skin with needles.

Taxidermy The art of stuffing and mounting animals so that they are preserved and look like live animals.

Theory An idea, especially one based on scientific study, that is used to explain how or why something happend.

Whalers Fishermen who hunt whales for their meat and the valuable oil it contains.

Finding Out More

Visiting a museum is a good way to find out more about the natural world and the way plants and animals have slowly changed. The Museum of Natural History in New York and the Smithsonian Institute in Washington, D.C. have full-sized dinosaur skeletons as well as many stuffed animals similar to the specimens Darwin sent back to England. If you do not live near these cities, visit your local museum; many have a natural history section.

Books to Read

Your local library should be able to help you find these books.

Charles Darwin, *On the Origin of the Species*
   Norton, 1975
Charles Darwin, *The Voyage of the Beagle*
   Doubleday, 1967

Picture Acknowledgments

The photographs and engravings in this book are provided by:
Barnaby's Picture Library 22; BBC Hulton Picture Library 5, 6, 24; Bruce Coleman Ltd 9, 10, 19, 20, 21, 24; Mary Evans 6, 13, 28, 29; The Mansell Collection 26; Oxford Scientific Films 11, 25; Robert Pickett 27. Other pictures have been taken from the Wayland Picture Library.

Index